WHAT'S WRONG BABY EVAN ?

Written By

Andrea N. Hardaway

Acknowledgements

Four years ago, God gave me the idea to write this book. I failed to do so for various reasons, doubt being number one, but through God's love and guidance I was able to complete to be obedient. I truly thank God for being patient with me in this journey and for placing people in my path that would help bring this book to life. Many thanks to my loving husband for encouraging and motivating me even before I decided to write this book. He has always believed in me when I didn't believe in myself. I thank God for blessing me with him. Special thanks to our little bundle of joy, Evan. This book would not have been possible had God not placed him in our lives. Evan has brought so much joy, excitement, and completion to our family. I would also like to thank Linda for sharing the information with us about becoming foster parents. Little did we know that we would be able to adopt him 2 years later. Thank you for being helpful, thoughtful, and concerned. Thanks to my dear and close friend Sherlette whom I've known for 21 years. You've always been there for me. I've enjoyed our conversations about God and how we uplift each other. I thank God for placing you in my life, and I thank you for introducing me to Mrs. Verna who assisted me on this journey to write my first book. Mrs. Verna, I really appreciate your help, patience, and understanding during this tedious process.

The doorbell rings and Mom opens the door. "Hello, Ms. Charlene. Thanks for bringing our new little bundle of joy, Baby Evan."

"He's got the sweetest little smile and the brightest little eyes, rosey cheeks, and his soft little hand is holding my pinky. I think he likes me already."

"Hello Baby Evan," Mom said. Baby Evan looks around as Mom takes him out of the car seat to hold him. Baby Evan smiles and moves his arms up and down. "How are you? Mommy is so happy to see you."

Mom hugs, kisses, and takes a picture of him. Baby Evan softly coos and gurgles. Then, Mom sends the picture to Daddy who is out-of-town on a school field trip.

Ring, Ring, Ring...

 "Hi Honey, did you see the picture of Baby Evan? Isn't he the cutest," said Mom. "That's my big boy," Dad said. "I can't wait to come home and play with him." Evan cries in the background. "I have to go now," said Mom. "Baby Evan is crying. We'll see you later."

"What's wrong Baby Evan? Are you sleepy, wet or hungry? Hmmm you're not wet. Maybe you are sleepy or hungry."

Mom feeds and burps Evan then rocks him in the rocking chair. Evan starts to cry again.

Waaa, Waaa, Waaa.

"Let's see, you're not sleepy, hungry or wet. What's wrong little fellow?" Evan looks, pouts, and cries even more. "No fever. Poor baby. Mommy doesn't know what's wrong with you. What could it be? What could it be?"

Evan continues to cry.

Mom holds Baby Evan, talks to him and calls daddy. "Hi Honey, Baby Evan is still crying." *Waaa, Waaa, Waaa...* "He is not wet, hungry, sick or sleepy. I checked his pamper, fed him, burped him and held him but he continues to cry."

"Good job Honey. You are catching on fast. Give him time to adjust. Remember this is new to him as well as us. We're leaving now. I should arrive home from Georgia later this evening. I can't wait to meet my big boy for the first time," said Dad. "Ok, we will see you then," said Mom. "I'm sure he's fine Honey. You are doing a great job," said Dad. "Thank you," Mom said. "We'll see you tonight."

"Baby Evan. What's wrong? Would you like to play on the floor and watch cartoons? Or would you like to look at a book about animals and the sounds they make? Let's look at the animal book."

"Wow! Evan would you look at that! Look at the dog, cat, and the duck." Baby Evan stops crying and looks at the pictures in the book. Baby Evan points to the dog and smiles. He stares at the cat and pouts. He then points to the picture of the duck and makes crying sounds with his mouth closed.

Mom begins to make the sounds of each animal.

"Look Evan. The dog says *Ruff, Ruff…*

The cat says Meow, meow...

The duck says *Quack Quack...*

Waaaa, Waaaa, Waaaa... cries Baby Evan. "Oh my, are you ok? Did that duckie scare you? Bad little duckie. It's ok, Mommy will protect you. Let's see which animal you like the most." Mommy points to each animal again and makes each sound. "Do you like the dog, *Ruff, Ruff?*"

Baby Evan smiles, gurgles and moves his little body back and forth.

"Do you like the cat, *Meow, Meow?*"

Baby Evan stares.

"Do you like the duck?"

Waaa, Waaa, Waaa...cries Baby Evan. "Well I think it's safe to say, you really like the little doggy. You're unsure of the cat but you certainly do not like the duckie."

"Mommy's going to put the animal book away, then let you play on the floor." Baby Evan watches Mommy as she puts the animal book away. Mommy then sits Baby Evan on the floor while she sits on the sofa.

Baby Evan falls over and continues to cry.

Waaa, Waaa, Waaa...

"Aww it's ok Baby Evan. Mommy's got you." Mommy holds Evan in her lap, bounces him, talks to him and sings.

Waaa, Waaa, Waaa...

Evan cries even louder! "Ok, ok, I'm sorry that Mommy's singing doesn't sound good. Oh sweetie, I wish you could tell me what's wrong."

"Mommy will just hold you and give you plenty of hugs and kisses." Baby Evan moves his head around then lays his head in Mommy's chest.

"Would you like a snack Baby Evan? Let's get a snack." Mommy places Baby Evan in his highchair. Then, she places the snacks on a plate in front of him. "Wow Evan, look at your yummy little snack, yummy yummy." Baby Evan reaches for his snack.

Baby Evan holds the snack in his hand, looks at it, places it on his nose, smiles and places the snack in his mouth. When he finished eating, he began to cry again.

"Evan, it's Daddy!" Evan wipes his eyes with his hand and looks at Mom. She hurriedly answers the phone, "Hi Honey," said Mom. "Hi, we're back," said Dad. "Can you come and get me please?" "Yes, we're on our way," said Mom.

23

Mommy secures Evan in his car seat and off they went. Baby Evan makes cooing sounds as he plays with his fingers and wiggles his toes. Mommy looks at Evan through the rearview mirror and notices how quiet and calm he is.

"Oh Evan, I see you're enjoying the car ride. Mommy's a great driver, isn't she?" Mommy and Evan arrive at daddy's school.

Daddy looks at Baby Evan through the car window for the first time. "That's my big boy, that's my big boy," said Dad. Evan sees Daddy for the first time and smiles. Daddy gets in the car and talks to him. Baby Evan smiles again and even laughs.

After they arrive home, Daddy and Evan play on the floor.

Evan laughs, smiles, waves his hands, and makes happy sounds. Mommy smiles and says, "Wow, Baby Evan really likes Daddy!" "Oh honey, Evan likes you too," said Dad. "He just wanted you to play with him on the floor!" "Yes, you're absolutely right," said Mom.

Mommy sits down to play with Evan and Daddy on the floor. "That's all he wanted! He just wanted me to play with him on the floor," said Mom.

"Oh Baby Evan, Mommy is so sorry. Now I know what was wrong. Thanks Love," said Mom. "No problem Honey," said Dad. "Now Daddy's going to teach his big boy how to crawl." Mommy, Daddy and Evan smile, laugh, and hug each other. What a wonderful start to our new loving family.

The End

Dedication

This book is dedicated to God for giving me the idea to write this book and the series that follows.

www.ingramcontent.com/pod-product-compliance
Lightning Source LLC
Chambersburg PA
CBHW042103040426
42448CB00002B/124